VERMONT

Past and Present

Michael Sommers

rosen publishing's
rosen central

New York

Published in 2011 by The Rosen Publishing Group, Inc.
29 East 21st Street, New York, NY 10010

Copyright © 2011 by The Rosen Publishing Group, Inc.

First Edition

Library of Congress Cataloging-in-Publication Data

Sommers, Michael.
Vermont: past and present / Michael Sommers. — 1st ed.
    p. cm. — (The United States: past and present)
Includes bibliographical references and index.
ISBN 978-1-4358-9498-3 (library binding) —
ISBN 978-1-4358-9525-6 (pbk) —
ISBN 978-1-4358-9559-1 (6-pack)
1. Vermont—Juvenile literature. I. Title.
F49.3.S67 2011
974.3—dc22

2009053185

Manufactured in Malaysia

CPSIA Compliance Information: Batch #S10YA: For further information, contact Rosen Publishing, New York, New York, at 1-800-237-9932.

On the cover: Top left: An engraving shows Vermont hero Ethan Allen surprising British troops at the Battle of Ticonderoga during the American Revolution. Top right: A Vermont dairy farm. Bottom: The city of Montpelier.

Contents

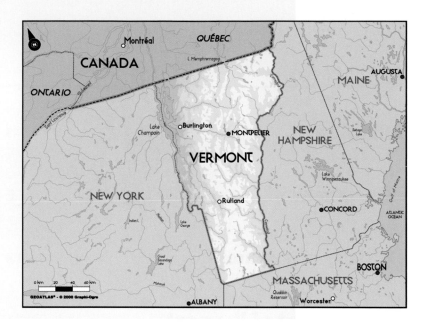

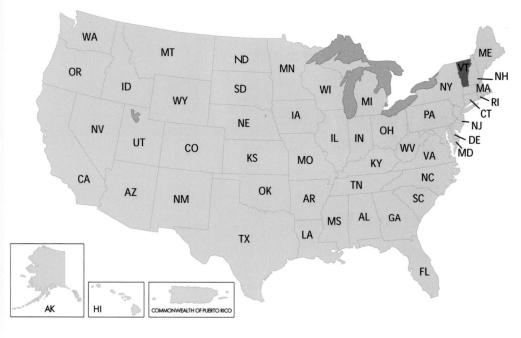

Located in New England, Vermont is known as the Green Mountain State. It is famous for its pristine wilderness, unspoiled forests, mountain peaks, and many rivers and streams.

Introduction

Vermont is home to large forests, rolling hills, and rugged mountains. With only a handful of cities and large towns, Vermont is a largely rural place where dairy and apple farms thrive. An increasing number of Vermont's many farms are organic, and their harvests go into the making of specialty food products. Vermont is the largest producer of marble and granite in the United States and has a number of software and communications companies.

When America first declared its independence from Britain, Vermont was refused membership as a state in the newly formed United States of America. Vermont became an independent republic with its own government—and even had its own postage stamps. To this day, the past remains strongly present in Vermont. It is reflected in the strong democratic traditions of Vermont's government, as well as the strong independent spirit of Vermonters themselves.

Vermont was the first state to outlaw slavery and the first state to guarantee the right to vote to all male residents over the age of twenty-one. It was also the first state that wasn't a former British colony. Vermonters protect their traditions, but never at the expense of progress. Fiercely independent, Vermont's men and women have always fought for their democratic rights as individuals and as citizens.

Chapter 1

The Geography of Vermont

Located in the northeastern tip of the United States, Vermont is the sixth-smallest state in the country. Shaped like a long rectangle that is wider at the top than at the bottom, its total area measures 9,614 square miles (24,900 square kilometers). One of America's smallest states in terms of size and population, Vermont is bordered by New York to the west, New Hampshire to the east, and Massachusetts to the south. The Canadian province of Quebec borders Vermont to the north. Lake Champlain, the sixth-largest lake in North America, is located along the border that Vermont shares with New York. The Connecticut River provides a natural border between Vermont and New Hampshire.

Vermont's Geographical Regions

Despite being a small state, Vermont boasts a surprising diversity of landscapes. The state is filled with high mountain peaks, fertile river valleys, and more than four hundred lakes, rivers, and streams. Vermont can be divided into six distinctive geographical regions: the Champlain Valley, the Green Mountains, the Taconic Mountains, the Vermont Valley, the Vermont Piedmont, and the Northeast Highlands.

The Champlain Valley

The Champlain Valley is a flat and fertile region located in northwestern Vermont. Its gently rolling land and nutrient-packed soil make it ideal for agriculture. Corn, hay, and oats are grown in the valley. Many of Vermont's apple orchards and dairy farms are located here as well. Squeezed between Lake Champlain to the west and the Green Mountains to the east, the valley possesses a mild climate. Burlington, Vermont's largest city with a population of approximately thirty-nine thousand people, lies on the lake's shore. There are eighty islands of all sizes found in Lake Champlain.

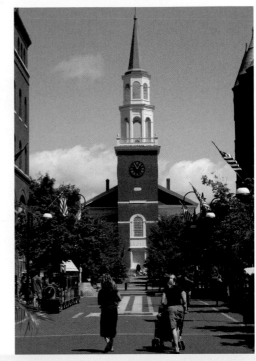

Located in the heart of Burlington, Church Street Marketplace is a series of historic streets and buildings that have been transformed into an open-air shopping mall.

The Green Mountains

The Green Mountains make up the spine of Vermont. Part of the Appalachian chain, these rocky peaks cut right through the middle of the state from Massachusetts up to the Canadian border. The Green Mountains are formed from rocks dating back some four hundred million years. Geologists believe that the mountains were originally 8,000 feet (2,438 meters) higher than they are today. Over time, a combination of wind, water, and ice wore them down while sculpting the rocks into spectacular shapes.

Vermont is famous for its vibrant fall foliage. Here, trees in the Green Mountains turn colors during autumn.

True to their name, the Green Mountains are covered in a thick carpet of trees. In the winter, however, the region's snow-covered peaks house popular ski resorts such as Stowe, Sugarbush, and Killington. Located in the north, the state's highest peak, Mount Mansfield, measures 4,393 feet (1,339 m). The southern part of the mountain range contains the Green Mountain National Forest. This 353,000-acre (142,965 hectares) patch of protected wilderness is popular with hikers, campers, and nature lovers.

The Taconic Mountains

Located in the southwest corner of Vermont, the Taconic Mountains also spill into New York and Massachusetts. However, the mountain range's highest peak, Mount Equinox, which measures 3,816 feet (1,163 m), lies within Vermont. Covered in forests, the mountains are rich in slate, shale, and marble. The lower hills are used as grazing pastures for dairy cattle.

The Vermont Valley

The narrow valley region located between the Green Mountains to the east and the Taconic Mountains to the west is known as the Vermont Valley. Many of Vermont's early settlements sprung up here, including the cities of Bennington, Manchester, and Rutland, the state's second-largest city. Otter Creek, the longest river in Vermont, flows through much of the valley and into Lake Champlain. Many of Vermont's famous marble quarries can be found in this region.

The Vermont Piedmont

The word "Piedmont" is French for "foot of the mountains." This region runs the length of Vermont, from Canada to Massachusetts. The Piedmont earned its name because the Green Mountains make up the region's western border. The largest of Vermont's six regions, the Piedmont consists of rolling foothills that gently slope down toward the Connecticut River and the New Hampshire border. The region is dotted with many lakes that were formed by melted glaciers. The Vermont Piedmont's lush countryside is ideal for agriculture, and it is also home to some of the state's most important granite quarries. Vermont's capital, Montpelier, is located here.

Lake Champlain

Lake Champlain has played an important role in North American history for centuries. Over the centuries, the lake has been a highway for the exchange of goods and served as a transportation route. The first people to settle along its shores were the Abenaki and Iroquois.

In colonial times, the lake was an essential transportation link between the St. Lawrence and Hudson valleys. In the eighteenth and nineteenth centuries, the lake served both military and commercial functions. The forts built along its shore were used during the American War of Independence, as well as during the War of 1812.

In 1823, the completion of the Champlain Canal, connecting Lake Champlain to the Hudson River, allowed goods and people to travel all the way from Canada to New York City. Through much of the nineteenth century, schooners and steamboats filled with cargo and passengers could be seen plowing through the lake's waters en route to the Atlantic Ocean. Since the mid-twentieth century, however, large ships have been scarce.

Today, the lake is used primarily for recreation. Covering an area of 435 square miles (1,130 sq km), with a maximum depth of approximately 400 feet (122 m), Lake Champlain is much smaller than any of the five Great Lakes. However, in 1998, it had a brief moment of greatness when President Bill Clinton signed a bill giving it Great Lake status. The resulting uproar was so great that the bill was suspended two weeks later.

Thousands of people flock to Lake Champlain every year. They are drawn by its great natural beauty, historical attractions, and the opportunities the lake offers for swimming, fishing, and boating. Lake Champlain is also noteworthy for a strange creature that some people claim to have seen in its waters. Much like the legendary Loch Ness Monster, this creature, nicknamed Champ is believed by some to be a gigantic reptile that has survived from prehistoric times. However, scientists remain unconvinced of Champ's existence.

The Northeast Highlands

A wild region known as the Northeast Highlands is located in the northeast corner of Vermont. The glaciers that once covered Vermont are responsible for carving out the Highlands' dramatic landscape, which consists of granite peaks mixed with low-lying lakes, bogs, and swamps. These geographic features, combined with rocky soil and a harsh winter climate, explain why this region is the least populated in the state. The beauty of the Highlands' pristine wilderness has earned the region the nickname of the Northeast Kingdom.

Trees and Forests

Around 78 percent of Vermont is covered in forests and woodlands. Vermont's most famous tree is the sugar maple. In the fall, its leaves turn scarlet red. The sap of sugar maples is used to make Vermont's famous maple syrup. Other deciduous trees—whose leaves also change color—include ash, beech, birch, and poplar. The vivid colors of Vermont's foliage during autumn are legendary and draw tourists from all over the country. Vermont also has many forests of coniferous trees, such as pine, fir, spruce, and cedar. Known as evergreens, these trees have needles that never fall off.

Wildlife

Vermont's forests and plains are home to a variety of wildlife. The most common large wild animal in Vermont is the white-tailed deer, but there are also moose and black bears. The state is home to small wild animals, such as beavers, foxes, muskrats, porcupines, raccoons, squirrels, wild rabbits, and woodchucks.

Vermont also shelters a great variety of avian specimens. Birds, including goldfinches, ruby-throated hummingbirds, and yellowthroats, add splashes of color to the landscape. Predatory birds, such as hawks, falcons, and owls, are common in Vermont, as are large non-flying birds, such as grouse and wild turkeys. The state's many lakes are home to ducks, geese, and loons, as well as many fish species, including bass, lake trout, northern pike, and yellow

Moose are a common sight in the fields and forests of northeastern Vermont. In fact, officials worry that there is a moose overpopulation problem in some regions.

perch. Atlantic salmon, brown trout, and rainbow trout live in Vermont's rivers, while brook trout inhabit colder mountain streams.

Climate

Like other New England states, Vermont has four distinct seasons. Winters are long and very cold with lots of snow. The coldest temperatures with the greatest snowfalls—something up to 10 feet (3 m) over the length of a single winter—are found in the mountains. Because winter lasts so long, spring is short and usually cool. Summer temperatures rarely climb above 90 degrees Fahrenheit (32 degrees Celsius). Days can be warm, while nights become chilly.

Chapter 2

THE HISTORY OF VERMONT

The first Native Americans to settle in the area that would become Vermont were the Abenaki people, who arrived between 1000 BCE and 1000 CE. In northern Vermont, the Abenaki built villages along the shores of Lake Champlain and the Missisquoi River. They planted crops, such as beans, corn, pumpkins, and squash. The Abenaki spoke Algonquin, a language common to various groups in the region with whom they traded goods.

Champlain and the French

The first European to arrive in Vermont was a French explorer and fur trader named Samuel de Champlain. Traveling south from Canada, Champlain journeyed to the large lake that today bears his name. Champlain claimed the lake and surrounding region in the name of the king of France. Vermont thus became part of the territory known as New France, which also included the French Canadian settlements of Montreal and Quebec.

French fur traders traveled into Vermont and set up trading posts where they could exchange wares, such as pots, blankets, jewelry, and guns for furs harvested by the Abenaki. The Abenaki, in turn, used the guns to expel their rivals, the Iroquois.

A number of streets, monuments, and natural landmarks in Canada and the northeastern United States are named after Samuel de Champlain.

However, the Iroquois weren't easily driven off. They continued to trap beavers so that they could supply fur to the newcomers—the English. In the mid-1600s, the English had begun to settle the colonies of Massachusetts, New Hampshire, and New York. In response, the French constructed a military post called Fort St. Anne on Lake Champlain's Isle La Motte in 1666. The fort became the first European settlement in Vermont. Defending the lake from the English and Iroquois was essential to the French. Navigating the lake was the only way that precious furs and other goods could be transported between French trading posts in Vermont and settlements in French Canada.

The French and Indian War

The English also wanted control of Lake Champlain. In 1724, they built a fort to the west of the Connecticut River. This fort, Fort Dummer, was the first English settlement in Vermont. Over the years, the rivalry that pitted the French and Abenaki against the English and their Iroquois allies grew. Although they once fought over fur trading territory, they now fought over who would control and settle the territories of the New World.

The conflict came to a head in 1754 with the French and Indian War. Ultimately, the English and the Iroquois defeated the French and the Abenaki. English victory was officially declared in the Treaty of Paris, which was signed in 1763. The treaty awarded all of France's North American colonies east of the Mississippi River, including Vermont, to England.

Revolt and Revolution

No sooner had Vermont come under English control than the English colonies of New York and New Hampshire started fighting over the right to settle the new territory. Before the French and Indian War, King George II of England had given the governor of New Hampshire the right to give settlers parcels of land. The land that was granted to the settlers had to lie to the west of New Hampshire. At the same time, the governor of New York was also giving settlers grants to the land east of New York.

In 1770, in an attempt to resolve this conflict, the king declared that the land belonged to New York. The furious New Hampshire settlers took matters into their own hands. In 1775, a Vermont farmer named Ethan Allen put together a small army of volunteers. Known as the Green Mountain Boys, this fierce band of two hundred men chased the New York settlers out of Vermont and took back their land.

In 1775, the first battles of the American Revolution broke out. American colonists fought against British soldiers for their

This nineteenth-century engraving depicts the Battle of Bennington. In this 1777 battle, which was named after the town of Bennington, Vermont, General John Stark led American troops to victory over the British.

independence. Ethan Allen and the Green Mountain Boys were involved in one of the war's first conflicts when they helped seize the British-held Fort Ticonderoga, which was located on Lake Champlain.

Vermont Becomes a State

Due to the land disputes between New York and New Hampshire, Vermont was not among the thirteen original American states. On January 14, 1777, however, Vermont declared itself a republic. Like an independent nation, the republic of Vermont had its own government. It was headed by a democratically elected president and governed according to laws drawn up in Vermont's constitution. Although the U.S. Congress accepted the new republic, New York and New Hampshire still claimed that they had rights to Vermont's territories. The conflict was settled in 1790, when Vermont paid the sum of $30,000 for the land it had taken by force. In 1791, Vermont became the fourteenth state of the United States.

Nineteenth-Century Vermont

Throughout the early 1800s, Vermont's population grew and the state prospered. People flocked to Vermont to start farms and work in the state's mills and quarries. Waterways, such as the Connecticut River and Lake Champlain, became important transportation routes.

When the Civil War (1861–1865) broke out, Vermont was the first northern state to send soldiers to fight with the Union army. In total, thirty-five thousand Vermont troops participated in the war. As the nineteenth century drew to a close, industry was thriving in and around the large cities of the northeastern United States. While some Vermonters migrated to cities in search of work in new factories, others sought jobs in Vermont's growing woodworking, cheese making, and tool making industries.

Disaster and Depression

Vermont experienced tough times in the early twentieth century. In 1927, the worst natural disaster in the state's history occurred when record rainfalls caused many of Vermont's rivers to flood. Eighty-five people lost their lives. Shortly after this, a second disaster occurred. This time, the disaster was a financial one. In 1929, the U.S. stock

Vermont's Population

With a population of about 623,050 (according to 2005 U.S. Census statistics), Vermont is the second least-populated state in the United States. Nonetheless, it has certainly grown since the first U.S. Census of 1790, when the state had a population of only 85,425.

In the early 1800s, the Irish came to Vermont to build the state's railroads. The development of the state's rock quarries in the mid-1800s lured Italian and Scottish immigrants to the state. Many German immigrants came to work in manufacturing industries in the late 1800s. In the later 1800s and until the 1960s, Vermont's population grew very slowly. The number of people who left Vermont was greater than the number that migrated to the state. To this day, Vermont is the most rural of all the states: At the dawn of the twenty-first century, more than two-thirds of Vermonters lived in communities with populations of less than 2,500 people.

In present-day Vermont, more than 23 percent of the population has French or French Canadian ancestry. More than 18 percent of the population having French and English ancestry can trace their roots back to the state's earliest days as a colony. Over 16 percent of Vermonters claim Irish descent, 6.4 percent are of Italian extraction, 4.6 percent are descended from Scottish immigrants, and 9.1 percent are descended from German immigrants. However, more and more new people are settling in Vermont. According to the U.S. Census Bureau, the state population increased by 2.3 percent between 2000 and 2005. Half of this increase was due to the arrival of new inhabitants: Around 50 percent moved from other states, while the other 50 percent emigrated from other countries.

Tragically, of the approximately ten thousand Abenaki who lived in Vermont prior to the arrival of European settlers, there are now fewer than 1,600 in the state. According to the U.S. Census, less than 0.5 percent of Vermonters have Native American ancestry.

market crashed, sending the country into a deep economic crisis known as the Great Depression. During the Great Depression, many Vermonters lost their jobs, their savings, and even their homes. To help create new jobs, the U.S. government launched public works projects. In Vermont, roads, dams, parks, and even ski trails were built by thousands of otherwise unemployed Vermonters.

World War II and Vermont's Big Boom

The Great Depression came to an end with the outbreak of World War II. The United States entered the war in December 1941. Industries ramped up production to satisfy the needs of the military. Many Vermonters sought jobs in the factories of neighboring states. With so many American men off fighting, women entered the workforce in record numbers. Between 1941 and the war's end in 1945, fifty thousand Vermonters fought for their country, and twelve thousand died.

After the war, the United States enjoyed a period of great prosperity. Vermont's population grew as people were attracted to the new jobs available in the state, and tourism boomed. In the 1960s and 1970s, a "back to the land" movement brought many people who were in search of a simpler, healthier life to settle in the small towns and countryside of Vermont.

Vermont Today

While the growth and development of the last few decades have generally been good for Vermont's economy, they've also had negative effects. Some of these drawbacks have included unchecked urban growth, pollution, and threats to the environment. As early as 1970,

Overlooking Lake Champlain Valley, Mount Philo State Park is only one of the many natural parks scattered throughout Vermont. The oldest state park in Vermont, it covers about 168 acres (68 hectares).

Vermont's government passed the Environmental Control Law, which permits land developers to proceed with building projects only if they can first prove that the project will not have any harmful effects on the environment. Vermont was the first state in the United States to pass such a law. In 1988, the state government followed up with the Growth Management Act, which protects the state's natural resources and parklands. Despite these conflicts between progress and preservation, the state remains the most rural in the United States.

Chapter 3

THE GOVERNMENT OF VERMONT

When Vermont became a republic in 1777, its first government drew up a constitution. This constitution outlined Vermont's basic laws and values. The constitution underwent changes in 1786 and in 1793, two years after Vermont became a state.

Vermonters have always valued liberty and democracy, and as a result, Vermont has always been a forward-thinking place. The 1777 constitution not only established Vermont as a state—it also outlawed slavery. Vermont was the first state in the country to do so. It was also the first state to guarantee all male residents over the age of twenty-one the right to vote. Although the current Vermont constitution is based on the constitution that was drafted in 1793, changes known as amendments have been added to it over the years. Amendments to the state constitution ensure that Vermont keeps up with the changing times.

Amendments can only be proposed once every four years by Vermont's legislature. Consisting of two houses, the senate and the house of representatives, the legislature is the branch of the government that creates new laws. A majority of both houses must approve an amendment for it to pass. They must then confirm their approval two years later. Once the amendment has been finalized by the government, the people of Vermont have their say. If the majority of citizens vote "yes" on the amendment, it is added to the constitution.

Vermont's Three Branches of Government

Much like the federal government, Vermont's state government has three branches: The executive branch, the legislative branch, and the judicial branch. These branches of government have a series of checks and balances so that no one branch can become more powerful than the others. Having three government branches that share power is a way of ensuring democracy.

Executive Branch

The executive branch is in charge of governing Vermont according to the laws of the state. The head of the executive branch is the governor. Governors are up for reelection every two years. Vermont's lieutenant governor, secretary of state, attorney general, and treasurer are also up for election every two years. There are no term limits on any of these positions. This means that an official in any of these positions can serve as long as he or she keeps getting reelected.

Legislative Branch

The legislature is responsible for creating state laws. The legislature, which is also known as the general assembly, consists of the senate and the house of representatives. Like members of the executive branch, state representatives and senators are elected by Vermonters every two years. Sessions in which they create, discuss, and pass bills into law take place between January and April, although the governor can call them to meet at any time throughout the year.

House Speaker Shap Smith closes a legislative session in Montpelier's historic State House on May 9, 2009. The State House was built in 1859.

Judicial Branch

The Vermont government's judicial branch consists of the state's court system. The highest court in Vermont is the state supreme court. It is presided over by a chief justice and four associate justices, all of whom are elected by the legislature to six-year terms. The supreme court's role is to interpret state law. Often, disagreements emerge in lower courts. People who feel laws haven't been applied justly appeal to the state supreme court. As the highest court in the state, it has the final word.

Vermont also has several lower courts. For instance, each of the state's fourteen counties has a superior court. These courts deal with

Democracy in Vermont

Originally, every town in Vermont elected a representative to the house of representatives. This tradition meant that by the time the twentieth century rolled around, there were an excessive number of representatives sitting in the State House. Although Vermont only has nine cities, it has 246 towns of less than 100 residents. In 1965, a federal judge decided that not every town in Vermont would get its own representative. As a result, the number of representatives plummeted from 246 to 150.

Although not every town has its own representative, it is still possible for politically minded citizens to take part in town meetings. Held every March (usually on the first Tuesday), these meetings allow all citizens to come together to elect town officials, vote on budgets for community projects, and discuss important issues. In fact, the first Tuesday in March has become known as Town Meeting Day.

This tradition of holding town meetings dates back to before Vermont was even a state; the first town meeting was held in Bennington in 1762. Back then, major issues put to vote included what agricultural goods citizens could use to pay their taxes, and issues related to the community. Town meetings served an important social as well as political function. They allowed Vermonters who might not know each other to meet and work together to solve problems that affected their community. Today, town meetings are much the same as they were more than 100 years ago. However, while the meetings may not have changed much over the centuries, the problems certainly have. Contemporary Vermonters can vote on pressing issues that affect their communities. For instance, they can vote on whether their taxes should pay for a youth center or a homeless shelter. Town meetings also allow Vermonters to discuss important topics that affect the entire state.

civil cases, which involve disputes about citizens' rights. Citizens who believe that they have been treated unjustly by a person or a business can take their case to a superior court to demand justice.

Each county in Vermont also has a district court. District courts typically hear criminal cases, or cases in which a defendant is accused of breaking a state law. A state attorney, or a lawyer who is representing the

A lawyer presents a case before the justices of Vermont's supreme court in October 2006. The supreme court building was constructed in 1918.

interests of Vermont's government, is in charge of prosecuting the accused. The district courts also hear some civil cases.

Each county has courts that deal with other types of legal problems. Family courts deal with cases concerning marriage, divorce, child support payments, and child abuse. Probate courts deal with estates, or the property people leave behind when they die. Vermont even has a special environmental court. The job of the court's only judge is to hear cases involving the protection of Vermont's environment and wildlife.

The State Capital

Vermont's capital, Montpelier, lies in a valley in central Vermont along the Winooski River. Its location in the heart of the state was

The Vermont State House in Montpelier can be seen for miles due to its glittering dome, which is covered with a thin layer of gold leaf.

the reason this small town with a population of 1,200 became the capital in 1805. In terms of population, Montpelier is still the smallest of all the U.S. state capitals. Currently, the town has only eight thousand inhabitants.

The executive and legislative branches of Vermont's government are based in Montpelier's historic State House, built in 1859. The governor and lieutenant governor have their offices here. The State House also contains the chambers of the house of representatives and the senate. Carefully preserved, they are the oldest legislative chambers in their original condition in the United States.

Chapter 4

THE ECONOMY OF VERMONT

Vermont has traditionally had an agricultural economy. However, the majority of Vermonters today work in the service industry, which includes the state's important leisure and hospitality sectors. Farming is still important to Vermont's economy, and manufacturing plays a major role in the state economy as well. Vermont also has many small businesses, which make everything from high-tech computer software to handmade canoes.

Agriculture

In 1870, there were five times as many cows as people in Vermont, and dairy farming was the most important economic activity in the state. Today, dairy farming is no longer the center of Vermont's economy, and the number of dairy farms in the state has fallen from 11,000 in 1947 to less than 1,100 in 2007. The state's dairy farms produce milk, cream, and butter. Vermont is also known for its cheeses. Mozzarella is the state's most commonly produced cheese, but aged Vermont cheddar is the most famous. Fresh Vermont eggs and milk are also ingredients in one of North America's most popular desserts: Ben & Jerry's ice cream.

A couple collects sap from the maple trees in their yard near Brattleboro, Vermont. The sap will be boiled down in order to make maple syrup.

Aside from dairy cows, Vermont farmers also raise beef cattle, chickens, pigs, and sheep. Corn and oats are grown as food for both animals and humans. Potatoes are one of the major state crops, and apples are Vermont's most widespread fruit.

Vermont produces more maple syrup than any other state. In the Champlain Valley, beekeepers raise clover-fed bees that produce excellent honey. The state is also home to a growing number of organic farms (in 2009, there were more than 500), where fruits and vegetables are grown without the use of chemicals and where animals are fed only natural foods. Today, more than 20 percent of all vegetable and dairy farms in Vermont are organic.

Mining

Mining has long been an important activity in Vermont. Although New Hampshire is known as the Granite State, Vermont is the foremost supplier of granite for buildings and monuments in the United States. The largest granite quarry in the country is the Rock of Ages quarry located near the town of Barre. Gray granite from Barre is used in 30 percent of the gravestones made in America and is used in building construction.

Vermont is also the country's biggest source of slate, which comes from the Taconic Mountains. Sheets of slate are used for floor tiles and roofing shingles. Other minerals that come from Vermont's quarries include limestone, which is also used in buildings, and talc, the main ingredient in talcum powder.

Manufacturing

The largest employer in Vermont's manufacturing industry is the computer and electronics giant IBM. In 2007, IBM was responsible for 25 percent of all manufacturing jobs in the state. Many high-tech companies that make computers, software, and electronics are located in and around Burlington.

Due to the needs of the state's mines and quarries, tools and mechanical equipment have been produced in Vermont for decades. The state also produces wood products, such as furniture, and paper products.

Tourism

Vermont's second-biggest industry is tourism. When the weather is warm, Vermont's many lakes and rivers beckon fishing enthusiasts,

Marble Quarries

Vermont has long been famous for its marble. In 1785, the first marble quarry in the country was opened by a Vermonter named Isaac Underhill in East Dorset. The nearby city of Rutland is perched right on top of large marble deposits. During the mid-1800s, thousands of quarry workers and stonecutters migrated to Rutland, earning it the nickname Marble City. During the early twentieth century, the Vermont Marble Company in nearby Proctor was the largest American corporation in the world.

Today, Isaac Underhill's Dorset quarry has been transformed into a swimming pool, and the Vermont Marble Company has been converted into the Vermont Marble Museum. Meanwhile, Vermont is still the largest producer of marble in the United States. The Vermont Danby quarry, which has been in operation for more than 100 years, is the largest underground quarry in the world.

Vermont marble comes in an astonishing range of colors, including white, black, yellow, green, blue, gray, red, and pink. Some of the U.S. landmarks that were made using Vermont marble are the Supreme Court Building and the Jefferson Memorial in Washington, D.C., and the United Nations Building and Rockefeller Center in New York City. Vermont itself is overflowing with marble buildings and monuments. There is even a State of Vermont Marble Trail that allows marble lovers to take in more than 120 sights ranging from Proctor's Wilson Castle and Montpelier's beautiful State House, to the gravestones that mark the resting places of independence hero Ethan Allen and poet Robert Frost.

A block of marble is removed from Vermont's Danby quarry.

and its mountains appeal to hikers and rock climbers. Resorts, restaurants, and tourist-related businesses offer year-round job opportunities for Vermonters. During the warm weather, many farms are open to tourists. Vermont is also famous for its summer camps. In the fall, "leaf peepers" descend upon the forests to see the spectacle of leaves turning gold, orange, and crimson.

When the weather grows cold, Vermont becomes a winter wonderland. The state's ski resorts play host to downhill skiers from all over the world. Stowe, Sugarbush, Burke Mountain, Pico, and the largest resort of all, Killington, are some of the most popular destinations. Tourists also

Vermont has a number of famous ski slopes. Here, skiers compete in the finals of the 2001 Winter X Games, held at Mount Snow, Vermont.

enjoy cross-country skiing in Vermont. Snowboarding was invented in the town of Stratton. Those who feel the urge for more speed can hop on a snowmobile—Vermont has more than 6,000 miles (9,655 km) of snowmobile trails.

PEOPLE FROM VERMONT:
PAST AND PRESENT

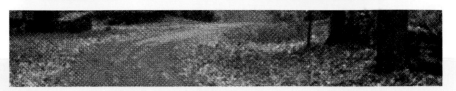

Chapter 5

Historically, Vermonters have cherished independence and free-thinking. It is no surprise, then, that some of the most famous men and women born in the state grew up to make important contributions to democracy both in Vermont and throughout the country. Meanwhile, the state's way of life and natural surroundings have inspired many writers and artists. Over the years, some have enjoyed Vermont so much that they chose to become permanent state residents.

Ethan Allen (1738–1789) Ethan Allen's passionate views and independent streak made him a natural leader of the Green Mountain Boys, a group of volunteer fighters who, in 1775, rose up against New Yorkers bent on settling Vermont. At the time, Allen proposed making the Vermont territory between Lake Champlain and the Connecticut River a free republic. Allen and the Green Mountain Boys were also responsible for capturing Fort Ticonderoga, a British fort strategically located on Lake Champlain, in one of the earliest important battles of the American Revolution.

Chester Alan Arthur (1829–1866) The son of a Baptist preacher, Chester Arthur was born in Fairfield. Before going into politics, he taught school, practiced law, and administered New York City's Custom House. Arthur was chosen to be John Garfield's vice president during the presidential elections of 1880. However, when Garfield was assassinated in 1881, Arthur became America's twenty-first president. He held this office until 1885. He helped pass important laws, such as the first federal immigration law, and a law guaranteeing the jobs of government workers no matter what their political beliefs.

Edna Beard (1877–1928) In 1920, Edna Beard of Orange, Vermont, became the first woman to be elected to the state's house of representatives. It was the same year that women won the right to vote. The first bill Beard enacted was to raise payments to single mothers. In 1923, Beard achieved another first when she was the first woman elected to the Vermont Senate. Her first successful bill allowed sheriffs to hire female deputies.

Calvin Coolidge (1872–1933) Born in Plymouth, Calvin Coolidge practiced law before being elected vice president in 1920. When President Warren G. Harding died of a sudden heart attack in 1923, Coolidge was sworn in as president. The U.S. economy prospered during Coolidge's presidency, and he was reelected in 1924.

John Deere (1837–1886) Born in Rutland, John Deere moved to Illinois to become a farmer. To break and turn the heavy soil of the Midwest, Deere invented a new type of plow made of cast-iron steel. The first model he created used

Women's Rights in Vermont

Throughout history, many notable Vermont women have fought for independence and equal rights. In the eighteenth and nineteenth centuries, Vermont women struggled to be treated as full citizens. They demanded the same rights that were accorded to men, such as the rights to vote, own property, and get a university education.

In 1785, Lucy Terry Prince, a former slave and one of America's first African American poets, appeared before the Vermont governor to defend her family's right to their own property in Guilford. In 1852, Clarina Howard Nichols, a journalist and women's rights advocate, was the first woman to address the Vermont Legislature. She asked for—and was denied—the right for women to vote at school meetings. In 1899, Mary Annette Anderson, of Shoreham, became the first African American woman to earn a college degree from Middlebury College. She graduated as class valedictorian. In 1910, Addie Card, a twelve-year-old cotton mill worker from Pownal, had her picture taken. This photograph, taken by a man named Lewis Hines, made her famous. She became a poster child for people who were fighting to end child labor.

In 1954, Consuelo Northrop Bailey was the first woman in the United States to be elected as a lieutenant governor. In 1933, Bailey had been the first woman allowed to practice law before the U.S. Supreme Court. In 1984, Madeleine Kunin became the first woman to be elected governor of Vermont, a post she held for three terms.

Today, advances in women's rights continue to be made in Vermont. In 1990, Denise Johnson was the first woman to serve on Vermont's Supreme Court, while Lavinia Bright became the first African American woman to be elected to Vermont's House of Representatives. In 1998, Deborah Markowitz became the first woman elected as Vermont's secretary of state. In 2001, April Rushlow was elected as chief of Vermont's surviving Abenaki tribe. Only thirty-three when she was elected, Rushlow is the group's first female chief.

the blade from a broken saw. By 1855, his factory was selling more than ten thousand plows a year. Today, John Deere is a company that makes and sells farming equipment around the world.

John Dewey (1859–1952)

Born in Burlington, John Dewey attended the University of Vermont before going on to become an important philosopher, psychologist, and educator. Dewey believed strongly in the importance of education for all Americans, and in citizens being informed so that they could exercise their democratic rights. During the early twentieth century, Dewey's views and writings were a major influence on public education.

Before starting his own company, John Deere spent his teens and twenties working as a blacksmith in Vermont.

Dorothy Canfield Fisher (1879–1958) Although she was born in Lawrence, Kansas, Dorothy Canfield Fisher lived most of her adult life in Arlington. A great believer in education, Fisher was a pioneer in introducing the Montessori method of teaching children in the United States. She also started the country's first adult education program. She was a best-selling author, and most of her novels and short stories were set in rural Vermont.

This 1942 portrait of Dorothy Canfield Fisher shows her attending a lunch for the Book of the Month Club. This club helps promote reading in the United States.

Robert Frost (1874–1963)

One of America's most respected poets, Robert Frost grew up and lived much of his life in Vermont. In 1920, Frost owned five farms there, but much of his poetry was written in a log cabin in Ripton, amid the Green Mountain National Forest. The winner of four Pulitzer Prizes for poetry, Frost read a poem that he composed at President John F. Kennedy's 1961 inauguration. In 1983, the governor of Vermont designated the area around Ripton as Robert Frost Country.

William Morris Hunt (1824–1879) Born in Brattleboro, William Morris Hunt came from a wealthy landowning family. When Hunt was a child, his father banned him from doing any art. Despite this, he grew up to be one of the most

important American painters
of the nineteenth century.
After his father died, his
mother took him to study art
at the finest schools in Europe.
When Hunt returned to the
United States ten years later,
he set up an art school in
Brattleboro. Later, he moved to
Boston, where he became
famous as a portrait painter.

John Irving (1942–) One of
America's best-loved fiction
writers, John Irving was born
in New Hampshire but has
lived much of his life in
Vermont. A teenage book-
worm, Irving grew up to
become a professor at

Novelist John Irving is seen here in a
1989 photo. Irving has a strong work
ethic—he spends up to eight hours a
day writing.

Windham College in Putney. Since 1967, he has lived all over
the state. His current home is in Dorset. Among Irving's most
popular novels are *The World According to Garp* (1978) and
The Cider House Rules (1985), both of which were made into
Hollywood films. Many of Irving's novels are set in New
England.

Bill Koch (1955–) Bill Koch is considered one of the greatest cold-weather endurance athletes. Born in Brattleboro,

Koch grew up in ski country. Despite suffering from asthma, he became one of America's top cross-country skiers. In 1976, he was the first American to win an Olympic medal for the sport when he took home a silver medal for the 18-mile (30 km) cross-country race.

Norman Rockwell (1894–1978) Originally from New York City, illustrator Norman Rockwell spent years living in Arlington, Vermont. Many of Rockwell's classic scenes of everyday American life were inspired by small-town Vermont life of the 1940s and 1950s. Moreover, many of the people in his paintings were based on the Arlington locals who posed for him.

Timeline

8500–7000 BCE Glacial activity creates the Champlain Sea.

1000 BCE–1600 CE Native Americans establish villages in Vermont.

1609	French explorer Samuel de Champlain discovers Lake Champlain and claims Vermont for France.
1666	The French build Fort St. Anne on Isle La Motte.
1724	British settlers build Fort Dummer, Vermont's first permanent settlement.
1763	The French and Indian War ends in the Treaty of Paris, which grants Vermont to the English.
1770	The Green Mountain Boys organize themselves in defense of the New Hampshire land grants.
1775	Ethan Allen leads the Green Mountain Boys in their capture of Fort Ticonderoga.
1777	Vermont declares itself an independent republic on January 15 and adopts its first constitution.
1785	The nation's first marble quarry opens in East Dorset.
1791	Vermont becomes the fourteenth state.
1805	Montpelier is chosen as Vermont's capital.
1859	Montpelier's State House is built.
1911	The Vermont Bureau of Publicity becomes the nation's first tourist office.
1923	Calvin Coolidge becomes the president of the United States after the death of Warren G. Harding.
1927	Flooding of the Winooski River kills eighty-five people and is considered the state's worst natural disaster.
2005	Vermont's population reaches 623,050.
2009	Same-sex marriage is legalized in Vermont.

State motto:	"Freedom and Unity"
State capital:	Montpelier
State tree:	Sugar maple
State fruit:	Apple
State bird:	Hermit thrush
State flower:	Red clover
Statehood date and number:	March 4, 1791; fourteenth state
State nickname:	Green Mountain State
Total area and U.S. rank:	9,615 sq miles (24,900 sq km); forty-third-largest state
Population:	623,000
Highest elevation:	Mount Mansfield at 4,393 feet (1,340 m)
Lowest elevation:	Lake Champlain at 95 feet (29 m)
Major rivers:	Otter Creek Lamoille River, Missisquoi River, Winooski River
Major lakes:	Lake Bomoseen, Lake Champlain, Lake Memphremagog

State flag

State seal

Hottest temperature recorded: 105˚F (41˚C) at Vernon, July 4, 1911

Coldest temperature recorded: -50˚F (-46˚C) at Bloomfield, December 30, 1933

Origin of state name: In French, *vert* means "green" and *mont* means "mountain"; the Green Mountains (*les Monts Verts*) were originally named by French explorer Samuel de Champlain. In 1977, it was Dr. Thomas Young's idea to combine *vert* and *mont* into Vermont.

Chief agricultural products: Dairy products (milk and cheese), apples, maple syrup

Major industries: Mining (marble, granite, slate), machine tools, wood working and paper, computers and electronics

Hermit thrush

Red clover

GLOSSARY

advocate A person who speaks or writes in defense of another person or cause.

amendment An alteration or addition made to a bill or constitution.

assassinate To kill a person for his or her beliefs. Assassinations are usually carried out against political or religious figures.

bog An area of wet, spongy ground.

coniferous A type of tree that has needles, rather than leaves, as well as cones.

deciduous A type of tree with leaves that change color and fall off during autumn.

descendant An individual whose origins can be traced back to a specific person or group.

diversity Variety.

geologist A person who studies the origin, history, and structure of the earth.

glacier A large, slow-moving mass of ice.

granite A common light-colored and very hard rock that is used for buildings and monuments.

grant To give.

marble A form of limestone that comes in many colors. Marble can be polished so that it's very shiny and smooth. It is often used by sculptors and builders.

organic Grown with fertilizers or pesticides of natural origin, as opposed to manufactured chemical origin.

predator Any living creature that survives by preying on other living creatures.

pristine Clean, pure, untouched.

quarry An excavation or pit from which stone is obtained.

ramp up To increase.

republic A state in which the power lies with the people who elect leaders to represent them.

rural An area in the countryside, outside of cities.

stag An adult male deer.

strategic Of essential importance.

FOR MORE INFORMATION

Green Up Vermont

P.O. Box 1191

Montpelier, VT 05601-1191

(802) 229-4586

Web site: http://www.greenupvermont.org

Green Up Vermont is a community organization that encourages Vermonters of all ages and backgrounds to work together in taking care of the state.

Vermont Department of Tourism and Marketing

National Life Building

6th Floor

Montpelier, VT 05620-0501

(802) 828-3237

Web site: http://www.travel-vermont.com

The Department of Tourism and Marketing offers a wealth of information about every possible attraction, event, and activity throughout the Green Mountain State.

Vermont Farms Association

P.O. Box 6004

Rutland, VT 05702

(866) 348-FARM (348-3276)

Web site: http://www.vtfarms.org

The mission of this association is to educate the public about Vermont's rich agricultural traditions. The association invites people to visit working farms and interact with local farmers, as well as to participate in farming events held throughout the state.

Vermont Fish and Wildlife Department

103 South Main Street

Waterbury, VT 05671-0501

(802) 241-3700

Web site: http://www.vtfishandwildlife.com

The Fish and Wildlife Department protects the state's natural habitats, carries out research, and educates the public about Vermont's fish and wildlife.

Vermont Heritage Network

Wheeler House
University of Vermont
Burlington, VT 05405
(802) 656-3180
http://www.uvm.edu/~vhnet
The goal of the Vermont Heritage Network is to increase awareness and appreciation of Vermont's cultural heritage and historic architecture.

Vermont Historical Society

60 Washington Street
Barre, VT 05641-4209
(802) 479-8500
Web site: http://www.vermonthistory.org
The Vermont Historical Society is dedicated to preserving Vermont's history.

Vermont State Parks

103 South Main Street
Waterbury, VT 05671-0601
(802) 241.3655
Web site: http://www.vtstateparks.com
This department of state parks offers information about all of Vermont's natural parks.

Web Sites

Due to the changing nature of Internet links, Rosen Publishing has developed an online list of Web sites related to the subject of this book. This site is updated regularly. Please use this link to access the list:

http://www.rosenlinks.com/uspp/vtpp

FOR FURTHER READING

Abbott, Jacob. *Marco Paul's Voyages and Travels: Vermont.* Ann Arbor, MI: Scholarly Publishing Office, University of Michigan Library, 2006.

Amsell, Sherry. *Vermont Nature Guide.* Mount Kisco, NY: Pinto Press, 1998.

Canfield Fisher, Dorothy. *Understood Betsy.* New York, NY: Henry Holt & Company, 1999.

Czech, Jan. M. *Vermont.* Danbury, CT: Children's Press, 2008.

Dornfeld, Margaret. *Vermont.* New York, NY: Benchmark Books, 2005.

Elish, Dan. *Vermont.* New York, NY: Benchmark Books, 2005.

Gauthier, Gail. *The Hero of Ticonderoga.* New York, NY: Puffin, 2002.

Hayford James. *Knee Deep in Blazing Snow: Growing Up in Vermont.* Honesdale, PA: Boyds Mills, 2005.

Heinrichs, Ann. *Vermont.* Mankato, MN: Capstone, 2004.

Hurwitz, Johanna. *The Unsigned Valentine and Other Events in the Life of Emma Meade.* New York, NY: HarperCollins, 2006.

Ketchum, Lisa. *Where the Great Hawk Flies.* New York, NY: Clarion, 2005.

Lunn, Janet. *The Hollow Tree.* New York, NY: Puffin, 2002.

Mitchell, Joyce Slayton. *Knuckleboom Loaders Load Logs.* New York, NY: Overlook, 2003.

Raabe, Emily. *Ethan Allen: The Green Mountain Boys and Vermont's Path to Statehood.* New York, NY: PowerPlus Books, 2002.

Rappaport, Susanne. *Messages from a Small Town: Photographs Inside Pawlett, Vermont.* Middlebury, VT: Vermont Folklife Center, 2005.

Stein, R. Conrad. *Ethan Allen and the Green Mountain Boys.* Danbury CT: Children's Press, 2003.

Venezia, Mike. *Calvin Coolidge.* Danbury, CT: Children's Press, 2007.

Abenaki Nation. "History." Retrieved September 2009 (http://www.abenakination.org/history.html).

Czech, Jan M. *Vermont.* Danbury, CT: Children's Press, 2002.

Dorothy Canfield Fisher Children's Book Award. "Who Was DCF?" Retrieved September 2009 (http://www.dcfaward.org/Biography/index.htm).

Ethan Allen Homestead Museum. "A Short Biography of Ethan Allen." Retrieved September 2009 (http://www.ethanallenhomestead.org/A-Short-Biography-of-Ethan-Allen.html).

Heinrichs, Ann. *Vermont.* Mankato, MN: Capstone, 2004.

Kaplan, Robert D. "Robert Frost's Vermont." *New York Times,* September 1, 1991. Retrieved September 2009 (http://www.nytimes.com/1991/09/01/travel/robert-frost-s-vermont.html).

Lake Champlain Maritime Museum. "History." Retrieved September 2009 (http://www.lcmm.org/shipwrecks_history/history/history.htm).

Montpelier, Vermont. "History." Retrieved September 2009. (http://www.montpelier-vt.org/history/index.cfm).

O'Connor, Kevin. "Daughter of the Dawn." *Barre-Montpelier Times Argus,* January 11, 2003. Retrieved September 2009 (http://www.timesargus.com/apps/pbcs.dll/article?AID=/20030111/NEWS/301110370).

St. Michael's College. "The Physiographic Regions of Vermont." Retrieved September 2009 (http://academics.smcvt.edu/vtgeographic/textbook/physiographic/physiographic_regions_of_vermont.htm).

St. Michael's College. "The Population of Vermont." Retrieved September 2009. (http://academics.smcvt.edu/vtgeographic/textbook/population/population_of_vermont.htm).

Vermont Agency of Natural Resources. "Vermont's Forests: Growing, Changing." Retrieved September 2009 (http://www.anr.state.vt.us/Env99/vtforest.html).

Vermont Marble Museum. "Home Page." Retrieved September 2009 (http://www.vermontmarble.com).

Vermont Visitors' Network. "Vermont Fun Facts." Retrieved September 2009 (http://vermontvisitorsnetwork.com/vtfacts).

Vermont Women's History Project. "Home Page." Retrieved September 2009 (http://www.womenshistory.vermont.gov).

White House. "Biography of Calvin Coolidge." Retrieved September 2009 (http://www.whitehouse.gov/about/presidents/calvincoolidge/).

INDEX

About the Author

Michael Sommers was born in Texas and raised in Canada. After earning a bachelor's degree in English literature at McGill University in Montreal, Canada, he went on to complete a master's degree in history and civilizations from the École des Hautes Études en Sciences Sociales in Paris, France. For the last twenty years, he has worked as a writer and photographer and has written numerous books for Rosen Publishing.

Photo Credits

Cover (top left) Stock Montage/Getty Images; cover (top right) © www.istockphoto.com/ Greg Panosian; cover (bottom) Jeb-Wallace Brodeur/Getty Images; pp. 3, 6, 13, 21, 27, 32, 39 Ron and Patty Thomas/Getty Images; p. 4 © GeoAtlas; p. 7 © www.istockphoto.com/Doug Schneider; p. 8 © www.istockphoto.com/Denis Tangney Jr.; pp. 12, 20, 23, 25 © AP Images; p. 14 Library of Congress Prints and Photographs Division; p. 16 © The Granger Collection; p. 26 © www.istockphoto.com/Scott Eagle; p. 28 Robert F. Sisson/National Geographic/Getty Images; p. 30 B. Anthony Stewart/National Geographic/Getty Images; p. 31 Al Bello/ Allsport/Getty Images; p. 33 Wikipedia (http://en.wikipedia.org/wiki/John_Deere); p. 35 Herbert Gehr/Time Life Pictures/Getty Images; p. 40 (left) Courtesy of Robesus, Inc.; p. 41 (left) Steve Maslowski/Getty Images; p. 41 (right) © www.istockphoto.com

Designer: Les Kanturek; Photo Researcher: Marty Levick